Taekwondo

in Action

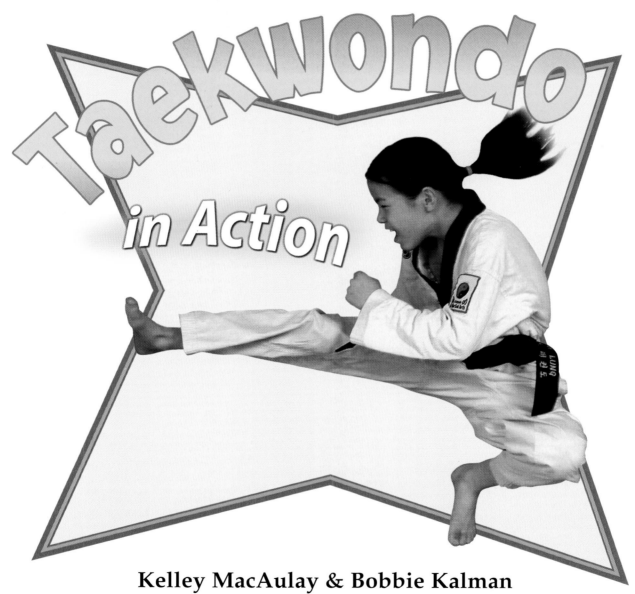

Kelley MacAulay & Bobbie Kalman

Photographs by Marc Crabtree

Crabtree Publishing Company

www.crabtreebooks.com

Created by Bobbie Kalman

Dedicated by Kelley MacAulay
For Rob MacAulay and Jennifer Black, with love

Editor-in-Chief
Bobbie Kalman

Writing team
Kelley MacAulay
Bobbie Kalman

Substantive editor
Amanda Bishop

Editors
Molly Aloian
Kristina Lundblad
Reagan Miller
Rebecca Sjonger
Kathryn Smithyman

Art director
Robert MacGregor

Design
Margaret Amy Reiach

Production coordinator
Katherine Kantor

Photo research
Crystal Foxton

Consultant
Jamie Hamilton, fourth degree black belt,
  Ahn Taekwondo Institute

Special thanks to
Victoria Lee, Tiffany Sue Lung, La Chaé Hood, Heather
McKee, Rajvinder (Robin) Singh, Ryan Coverdale, Alan
Bastien, and Seneca Tae Kwon-Do & Martial Arts

Photographs
All photographs by Marc Crabtree except:
Miguelez/Icon SMI: page 30

Illustrations
Katherine Kantor: chapter heading, pages 6, 12, 13, 20, 21,
  25, 29, 31
Trevor Morgan: page 7 (left)
Bonna Rouse: pages 7 (right), 8, 9

Crabtree Publishing Company

www.crabtreebooks.com   1-800-387-7650

Cataloging-in-Publication Data
MacAulay, Kelley.
  Taekwondo in action / Kelley MacAulay & Bobbie Kalman ; photographs
by Marc Crabtree.
    p. cm. -- (Sports in action)
  Includes index.
  ISBN 0-7787-0338-X (RLB) -- ISBN 0-7787-0358-4 (pbk.)
  1. Tae kwon do--Juvenile literature. [1. Tae kwon do.] I. Kalman, Bobbie.
II. Crabtree, Marc. III. Title. IV. Series.
  GV1114.9.M33 2004
  796.815'3--dc22
                                                    2004011121
                                                    LC

**Published in
the United States**

PMB16A
350 Fifth Ave.
Suite 3308
New York, NY
10118

**Published
in Canada**

616 Welland Ave.,
St. Catharines, Ontario,
Canada
L2M 5V6

**Published in the
United Kingdom**

73 Lime Walk
Headington
Oxford
OX3 7AD
United Kingdom

**Published
in Australia**

386 Mt. Alexander Rd.,
Ascot Vale (Melbourne)
VIC 3032

Contents

What is taekwondo?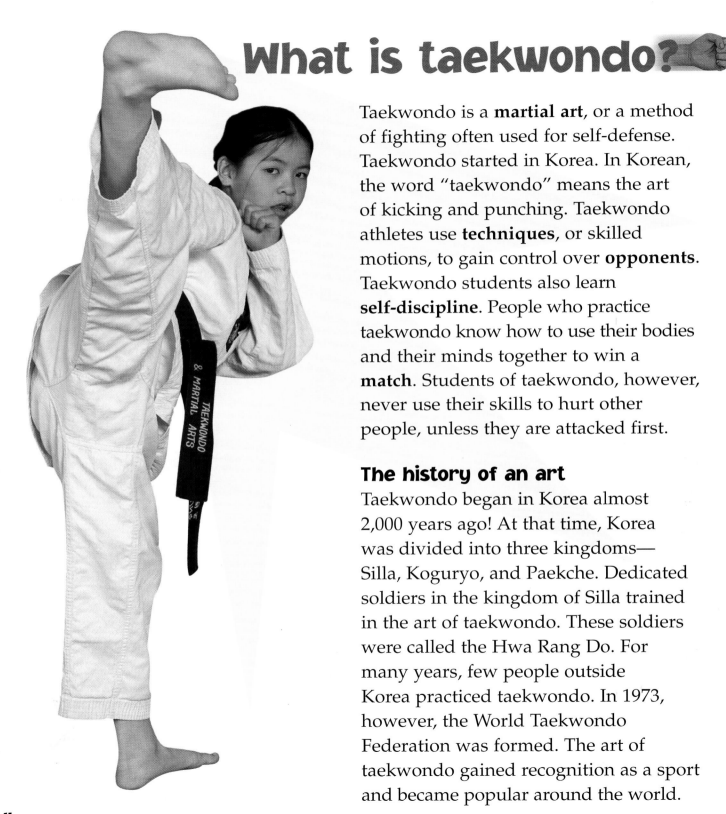

Taekwondo is a **martial art**, or a method of fighting often used for self-defense. Taekwondo started in Korea. In Korean, the word "taekwondo" means the art of kicking and punching. Taekwondo athletes use **techniques**, or skilled motions, to gain control over **opponents**. Taekwondo students also learn **self-discipline**. People who practice taekwondo know how to use their bodies and their minds together to win a **match**. Students of taekwondo, however, never use their skills to hurt other people, unless they are attacked first.

The history of an art

Taekwondo began in Korea almost 2,000 years ago! At that time, Korea was divided into three kingdoms—Silla, Koguryo, and Paekche. Dedicated soldiers in the kingdom of Silla trained in the art of taekwondo. These soldiers were called the Hwa Rang Do. For many years, few people outside Korea practiced taekwondo. In 1973, however, the World Taekwondo Federation was formed. The art of taekwondo gained recognition as a sport and became popular around the world.

Rules and respect

Respect is one of the most important elements of taekwondo. Students must show respect for their instructors, classmates, and **dojangs**, or training halls, by following a code of proper behavior. For example, when students enter or leave their dojangs, they bow to greet their instructors. Students also show their respect by arriving on time and by paying attention in class.

Personal best

Learning taekwondo is very challenging. It takes years of practice to become a **taekwondo master**. One way students gain skills and challenge themselves is by participating in competitions. Every student's main goal, however, is to perform his or her personal best every time. Winning a competition is not as important as competing fairly.

*The style of taekwondo that people practice today was greatly influenced by **karate**, a Japanese martial art.*

The essentials

Before you begin studying taekwondo, you must choose a dojang. Most dojangs belong to one of several taekwondo organizations. Each organization practices a different style of taekwondo.

The style taught at your dojang will depend on the organization to which it belongs. The style of taekwondo shown in this book is that of the World Taekwondo Federation.

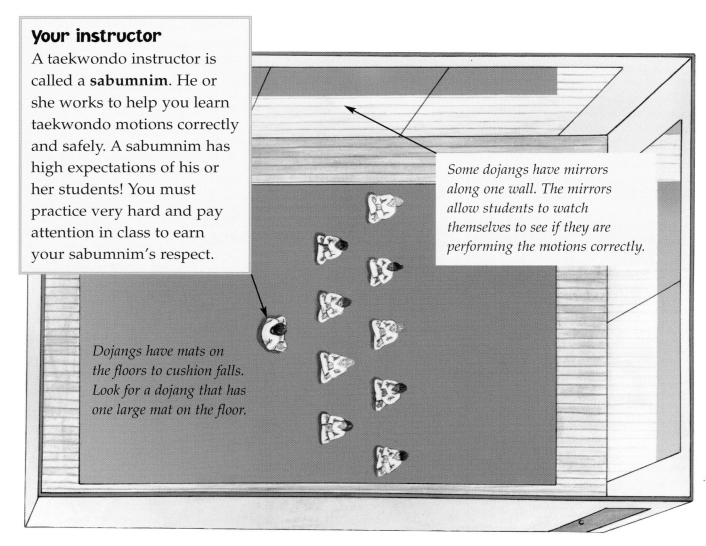

your instructor

A taekwondo instructor is called a **sabumnim**. He or she works to help you learn taekwondo motions correctly and safely. A sabumnim has high expectations of his or her students! You must practice very hard and pay attention in class to earn your sabumnim's respect.

Some dojangs have mirrors along one wall. The mirrors allow students to watch themselves to see if they are performing the motions correctly.

Dojangs have mats on the floors to cushion falls. Look for a dojang that has one large mat on the floor.

Suit up!

The only equipment you need as a taekwondo student is a traditional white uniform called a **dobok**. The dobok consists of a **tunic** and loose-fitting pants. Students train and compete in their doboks. It is important that they take good care of their uniforms. It is disrespectful to attend class in a dirty or torn dobok.

Before starting class, remember to tie back long hair and remove all jewelry. Also remember that chewing gum is not allowed in a dojang!

It is important to drink plenty of water while you practice or compete. Do not drink too much at once, however.

Earning your belts

A dobok is tied at the waist with a belt. Beginners wear white belts, which represent purity. Each time a student advances to the next level, he or she earns another belt. Students must pass tests to prove that they are ready to receive the next belt color. The first belt levels are called **gups**. The gup belts begin with the white belt and end with the red belt.

Black belts

Once students have earned all their gup belts, they can try for the first-level black belt. There are ten levels of black belts, called **dans**. Each requires higher skills and more experience in taekwondo.

Students do not wear shoes in the training area of their dojang.

white belt

yellow belt

green belt

blue belt

red belt

black belt

Warming up

Taekwondo challenges your body. To prevent injuries, your sabumnim begins each class with a series of warm-ups and strengthening exercises. Start by walking briskly for five minutes to get your heart pumping. Next, try some of the stretches shown on this page. Only stretch as far as you can without feeling pain. With practice, the stretches will become easier. Once you have stretched your muscles, try the strengthening exercises on the next page. Having strong muscles makes it easier to perform powerful kicks and strong punches.

"V" Stretch

Sit with your legs in a "V" position. **Flex** your feet so your toes are pointed upward. Keeping your lower back straight, lean forward until you feel a stretch in the back of your legs and buttocks. Hold the stretch for a count of ten.

Side splits

Slowly ease into the side splits by extending your legs as far to the sides as possible. Make sure the inside edges of your feet are on the floor. Place your hands on the floor in front of you and lean slightly forward. Hold this position for 20 seconds.

Quadriceps stretch

Stand on your left foot and lift up your right foot behind you until you can grab it with your right hand. Keep your knees together. You will feel a stretch in the front of your right leg. Hold the stretch for a count of ten and then switch legs.

Crunch "V"-sit

Sit with your legs stretched out in front of you and your hands behind your head. Keeping your knees together, pull your legs toward your chest and bring your upper body forward to meet them. Extend both legs until your body is in a "V" position. Do ten crunches.

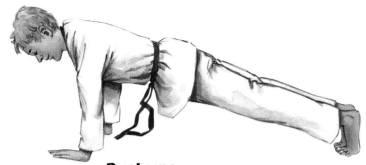

Pushups

Lie on your stomach. Place your hands flat on the floor beneath your shoulders. Use your arms to push yourself up. Be sure to keep your back flat. Lower yourself until your nose is about four inches (10 cm) from the mat. Repeat ten times. If you find the movement too difficult with your legs extended, try keeping your knees on the floor as you push up.

Mind and body as one

Your sabumnim may begin the class with a **meditation**, or an exercise to focus the mind. To meditate, sit quietly on the floor with your legs crossed. Close your eyes and breathe deeply, paying attention to every breath you take. When you meditate, your mind becomes focused on your body. Meditation helps you feel very relaxed and increases your ability to concentrate.

Positions, please

No matter how complex taekwondo motions are, they all start with basic positions. The first positions you learn are called **stances**. A stance is made up of the positions of your feet, legs, and upper body as you stand. If a stance is done properly, your legs and hips will not move, even if you move your upper body. A solid lower body position gives power to any technique you perform. If you practice your stances often, your balance and **coordination** will improve. You will also learn to move easily from one stance to the next. These pages show some of the basic stances that you will use over and over again.

Ready stance

Stand with your feet about shoulder-width apart. Bend your knees slightly. Close your hands into **fists** (see page 12) and hold them at belt level, with your elbows bent.

Horseback-riding stance

Stand with your legs spread twice as wide as the width of your shoulders. Point your feet forward and bend your knees. With your arms at your sides, close your hands into fists. Now quickly pull your elbows backward, until your hands are at belt level. The palms of your hands should be pointing upward.

Front stance

Stand in ready stance and take a large step back with your left foot. Bend your front knee until you can no longer see the toes of your front foot. Keep your back leg straight. Point your back foot forward. Extend your right arm above your right leg. Pull your left arm back to belt level, with your palm pointing upward.

Fighting stance

Stand in ready stance. Turn your feet slightly to the right and step back with your right foot. Your knees should be slightly bent. With your hands in fists, raise your arms until you are holding your fists in front of you.

Back stance

Stand in ready stance and take a large step back with your right foot. Turn your right foot until your toes are pointing to the side. Point your front foot forward. Bend your knees. Turn your upper body until it is pointing in the same direction as your back foot, but keep your head facing forward.

Before striking out

Taekwondo students use their hands and feet mainly to **strike**, or hit, their opponents. When students change the positions of their hands or feet, the motions have different effects. Each position creates a new **striking surface**, or part of the body that makes contact with the opponent.

Holding your hands and feet in the correct positions will make your motions effective and strong. It will also ensure that your motions are not painful to perform! The hand and foot positions shown on these pages will be useful when you perform many punches and kicks.

The fist is the most common hand position. To make a fist, curl your fingers into your palm and press your thumb against your first two fingers. To prevent injuries to your fingers, make sure they are closed very tightly. The knuckles on your fist provide the greatest striking power.

*An easy way to make your fist even more effective is with the **knuckle fist** position. Begin by making a fist. Push your middle finger forward so that the second knuckle sticks out beyond the other knuckles.*

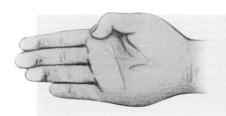

*To make the **knife hand** position, straighten your fingers and press them together. Then curl the tips of your fingers slightly inward to prevent them from being injured. Bend your thumb and press it against the inside edge of your hand. Use the outside edge of your hand to strike your opponent.*

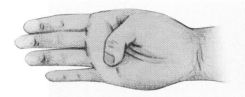

*To make the **spear hand** position, hold your fingers as you would to perform the knife hand position. Press your thumb against the inside of your palm. The striking area of the spear hand is at the tips of your fingers.*

Foot patrol

Unlike hand positions, foot positions do not have specific names. Instead, they are referred to by the area of the foot that is used. To control which part of your foot makes contact with your opponent, you need to bend your foot in a specific direction. The difficulty is getting your foot into position quickly enough and being able to hold that position upon impact.

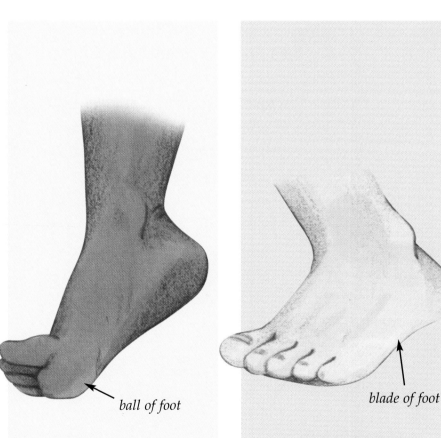

ball of foot

blade of foot

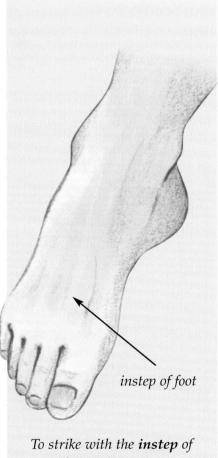

instep of foot

*To strike with the **ball** of your foot, bend your foot away from your knee while flexing your toes backward, toward your knee.*

*To strike with the **blade** of your foot, pull your foot toward your knee. Next, turn your foot until the outside edge is facing your opponent.*

*To strike with the **instep** of your foot, point your toes. Turn your foot until the top of your foot is facing your opponent.*

Packing a punch

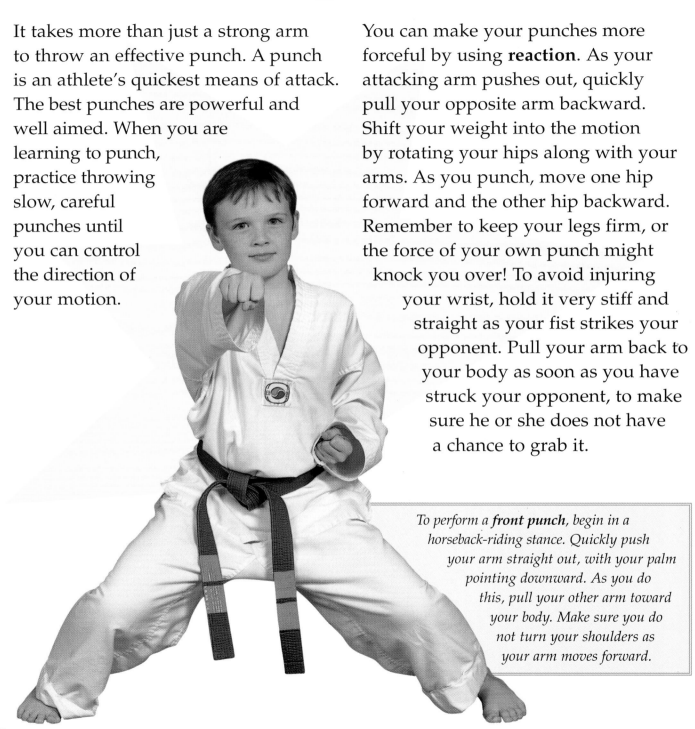

It takes more than just a strong arm to throw an effective punch. A punch is an athlete's quickest means of attack. The best punches are powerful and well aimed. When you are learning to punch, practice throwing slow, careful punches until you can control the direction of your motion.

You can make your punches more forceful by using **reaction**. As your attacking arm pushes out, quickly pull your opposite arm backward. Shift your weight into the motion by rotating your hips along with your arms. As you punch, move one hip forward and the other hip backward. Remember to keep your legs firm, or the force of your own punch might knock you over! To avoid injuring your wrist, hold it very stiff and straight as your fist strikes your opponent. Pull your arm back to your body as soon as you have struck your opponent, to make sure he or she does not have a chance to grab it.

*To perform a **front punch**, begin in a horseback-riding stance. Quickly push your arm straight out, with your palm pointing downward. As you do this, pull your other arm toward your body. Make sure you do not turn your shoulders as your arm moves forward.*

Knife hand strike

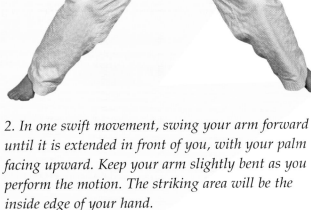

1. To perform a **knife hand strike**, begin in horseback-riding stance. With your hand in a knife hand position, raise your arm until your hand is close to the side of your head. Keep your palm turned away from your body.

2. In one swift movement, swing your arm forward until it is extended in front of you, with your palm facing upward. Keep your arm slightly bent as you perform the motion. The striking area will be the inside edge of your hand.

Express yourself

When taekwondo fighters are performing aggressive motions such as punches, they let out loud yells called **ki-haps**. To make the yell very loud, use your stomach muscles to push the yell out. The main reason to yell is to frighten or startle an opponent. Surprising an opponent gives you the opportunity to catch him or her off-guard. Letting out a loud yell also stirs up your own courage!

Kick it!

Taekwondo uses more kicks than does any other martial art. Kicks are more powerful than punches because the muscles in your legs are bigger and stronger than the muscles in your arms. Your legs are also longer than your arms, so kicks can be thrown from a safer distance than punches can be.

For kicks

Kicks are the most difficult taekwondo motions to master. They require coordination, balance, and aim. Your sabumnim will teach you how to concentrate while kicking. Concentration allows you to control your kicks and make them as effective as possible.

How to practice

Kicks require a lot of energy. If you get tired, you may lose your balance and give your opponent an advantage. It is important to practice kicks often to build **stamina**. **Double kicks** are good exercises for building strength. To perform a double kick, extend your leg twice before lowering it. Make sure you keep your knee as high as possible while doing a double kick. Holding your knee up during kicks will build strength in your leg and also help block your opponent's attacks.

*Try to perform as many kicks as you can each time you practice. If you can do a variety of kicks, you will be able to keep your opponent guessing about what your next move might be. This girl is performing a **roundhouse kick**.*

Step-by-step

1. The most powerful kick you can perform is the **side kick**. To perform a side kick, begin in fighting stance. Raise your back leg until your knee is at hip level. Turn the foot on which you are standing until it is pointing away from the direction at which your raised foot will strike out.

1. To perform a basic **front kick**, begin in fighting stance. Raise your back leg until your knee is level with your hip, bending your knee as you lift. Bend your foot away from your knee, while pulling your toes back toward your knee.

2. Quickly thrust your raised leg forward, holding the leg as high as possible.

2. Extend your foot upward and outward as fast as possible. Your striking surface is the heel of your foot.

Elbow strikes

Your hands and feet are not the only striking surfaces you can use to attack an opponent. Elbows can also be used to strike out in many directions. An **elbow strike** is a great self-defense technique when you find yourself very close to an opponent.

1. To perform a basic elbow strike, begin in front stance. Your back arm will be your striking arm. While keeping your striking arm bent, raise it until it is in front of your body, with your fist close to your chest.

2. To stabilize your striking arm, wrap your other hand around your fist. Keep your legs steady as you perform the motion. Shift your weight into the motion by turning your hips along with your elbow.

Fancy footwork

Before you begin performing more than one technique at a time, you will need to develop great **footwork**. Footwork is the series of steps you take while fighting. Good footwork allows you to control the distance between yourself and your opponent. Paying attention to your footwork will also keep you from tripping over your own feet! Once you feel comfortable using footwork, you'll be able to trick opponents by **feigning**, or faking, motions. To feign a motion, step in one direction and then quickly turn in another direction. The **Jeonjii step**, shown below, is simple footwork used to move forward while attacking.

1. To perform the Jeonjii step, begin in fighting stance. Slide your back foot forward until it is behind your front foot.

2. Next, slide your front foot forward until you are in fighting stance once again.

The old one-two

Once you have learned some different motions, you can try connecting them. A **combination** is a minimum of two basic techniques that are performed right after one another. Knowing how to link motions together is important—if you perform one motion and it fails, you have another one ready to go! Combinations are also impressive and useful techniques to use during competitions, when you must think faster than your opponent. For more information on competitions, see pages 30 to 31.

1. A good beginner combination is a front kick followed by a fast punch. Begin in fighting stance. Raise your back leg and perform a front kick.

Pulling it all together

There are different combinations from which to choose. Try out as many as you can until you learn which moves feel most natural to you. Combine moves that work well with your strengths. For example, if you are very flexible, you might want to focus on combining several kicks.

2. Throw your punch as soon as you place your foot back on the ground. An effective punch to throw from a fighting stance is the **reverse punch**. To perform a reverse punch, extend your back fist toward your target with as much force as possible.

Building blocks

As you practice taekwondo, you will learn to watch your opponent carefully. When you are able to determine which move he or she is going to make next, you can **block** the attack. A block is a defensive motion that stops a kick or punch from striking your body. A block can be performed with your hand, wrist, arm, elbow, knee, or foot. The block you use will depend on the part of your body the attacker is trying to strike. The goal of a block is not to stop the kick or punch altogether—that would be very difficult! Instead, you want to **deflect** the attack.

Duck!

Another way to avoid being struck is by **evading**, or moving your body out of the way. When evading an attack, it is important to move your body only as far as needed to avoid an opponent's motion. If you pull your body too far in one direction, you may lose your balance. It is a good idea to block an attack even when you try to evade it. If you don't move fast enough to evade, you can still deflect the attack.

*Follow every block with a quick **counterattack**. As you block your opponent's move, he or she may lose concentration for a moment. Such an opportunity would allow you to throw a swift punch or kick.*

Practice makes perfect

Basic blocks, such as the **low block**, the **rising block**, and the **knife hand block**, are very important moves in taekwondo. Practice each block with both your right hand and your left hand. If you can block successfully with each of your hands, you will be able to defend either side of your body. Practice your blocks until you can throw them with confidence.

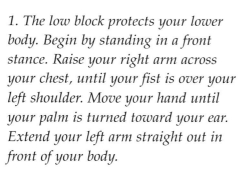

1. The low block protects your lower body. Begin by standing in a front stance. Raise your right arm across your chest, until your fist is over your left shoulder. Move your hand until your palm is turned toward your ear. Extend your left arm straight out in front of your body.

2. To block the attack, swing your right arm down until it is in front of your lower body. Your palm should be turned downward. As you move your right arm, pull your left arm in toward your body, with your palm facing upward.

23

Form and function

Taekwondo is not only about fighting. The artistic side of taekwondo is called **poomse** or **forms**. Forms are movements arranged in a specific pattern so they will flow into one another. A student must learn a new form to advance to the next belt level. As the belt levels become more advanced, additional techniques are added to the forms.

Forms should be performed gracefully. They require concentration and a lot of practice. Forms are not performed with a partner, but you should imagine an opponent as you practice. This will help you throw punches and kicks at the proper height. Forms take a long time to learn, but they help you become confident enough to combine motions and throw them from any direction.

Taegeuk

Some taekwondo organizations practice forms with different sets of movements. The World Taekwondo Federation uses a set of forms called **Taegeuk**. Below is the white-belt form in Taegeuk, which is called **Taegeuk Il Jang**.

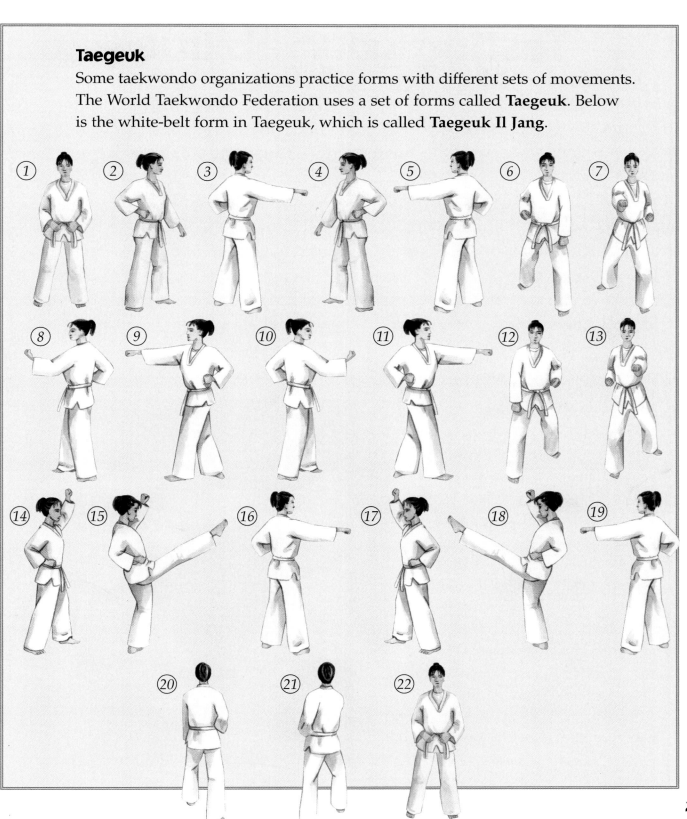

Testing your abilities

As your skills develop, you will want to try out your taekwondo motions with a real opponent. To do this safely, students must learn how to **spar**, or practice fight. Sparring is always supervised by a sabumnim. Sparring is one of the most important elements of taekwondo. It allows students to gain confidence in their fighting skills. It also helps them learn respect and fair play.

Styles of sparring

There are two main styles of sparring—**one-step sparring** and **free sparring** (see pages 28 to 29). In one-step sparring, students pair off to perform exercises using techniques that have been laid out by their sabumnim. The exercises teach students how to control the distance between themselves and their opponents and how to react quickly to attacks.

One step at a time

During a one-step sparring exercise, you and your opponent stand facing each other. The match begins after you bow to each other as a sign of respect. One student assumes the role of the attacker, and the other student acts in self-defense. The attacker takes a step toward the defender and performs a technique, such as a kick or a punch, which the defender blocks. The defender then performs a counterattack. Once you and your partner have performed the exercise a few times, switch roles.

Can't touch this!

At first, one-step sparring drills are **no-contact**. No-contact exercises are done slowly enough so students can stop their techniques right before they hit their opponents. As you practice no-contact drills, you will learn how to control your kicks or punches so you can throw them powerfully and not strike your opponent. Eventually, the exercises become **light-contact**, which means a fighter lightly strikes his or her opponent. To see some of the equipment needed for light-contact sparring, see page 29.

Keeping things fair

The body of a taekwondo student becomes powerful as he or she masters the art. It is very unsafe for a beginner to fight against an advanced student! To avoid accidents, fighters spar only against opponents of the same belt level, weight, and age.

The fight is on!

In free sparring, everything a student has learned about techniques, footwork, and timing comes together. Free sparring is done by advanced students. The fighters do not use set exercises as they do in one-step sparring, so they must think on their feet. The element of surprise makes free-sparring fights fast-paced and exciting to watch.

Following the rules

Students must follow many rules in order to create a safe environment for free-sparring fights. They are not allowed to attack certain areas of their opponents' bodies, including the neck, or any body part below the belt. It is also forbidden to strike an opponent's back. Free sparring is not simply a physical challenge, however. Students must control their tempers and show respect for their opponents. Pushing or grabbing an opponent out of anger is never acceptable!

Full-on fighting

Different schools allow varying degrees of contact during free-sparring matches. Students who are learning taekwondo for fun or exercise usually continue to practice light-contact sparring. Students who are interested in competitions, however, move on to **full-contact** sparring, which means they strike their opponents with full force. Full-contact sparring can be very dangerous, so students should try full-contact sparring only under the direction of their sabumnims. Full-contact sparring drills require students to wear protective gear including helmets, mouth guards, chest pads, leg and arm pads, and special pads to protect their hands and feet. Mouth guards are worn inside fighters' mouths. Leg and arm pads are worn under the doboks.

helmet

chest pad

hand pad

foot pad

Breaking techniques

Using **breaking techniques** is another way advanced taekwondo fighters test the control and power of their moves. To perform a breaking technique, a fighter strikes a sheet of wood, brick, or cement with his or her hand or foot. Fighters must have great focus in order to break their targets. Performing breaking techniques is an impressive accomplishment, but it is not part of a taekwondo student's regular training.

Competitions

Taking part in competitions is the ultimate test of a taekwondo student's abilities. Taekwondo competitions are popular because these events are very intense and energetic. During a competition, two fighters free spar with each other. A competitor scores points for every kick and punch that lands on a legal area of his or her opponent's body. To impress the judges, a fighter's movements need to be controlled, precise, and very powerful. Fighters score extra points for **knockdowns**, or attacks that cause their opponents to stagger or fall. A **knockout** attack can win a match. A knockout means that one competitor has fallen after an attack and cannot get up to continue the fight. Knockouts are not allowed in children's matches, however.

In 2000, taekwondo became an official sport at the Olympic Games in Sydney, Australia.

Keeping score

There are many people present at each competition to ensure that matches are safe and fair. The **referee**, or the person who controls the match, is in the **contest area** with the fighters. The referee declares the beginning and end of the match, gives out warnings to the fighters, awards and deducts points, and makes sure that the competitors are always safe while fighting. There are also four **judges**. One judge is positioned at each of the four corners of the ring. The judges record all points, deductions, and warnings given to the fighters. Each judge has a different view of the ring, so if the referee is not sure which fighter deserves a point, he or she can ask a judge for an opinion. The **jury** reviews the scores that the judges have awarded, to make sure all points were recorded correctly. After reviewing the score cards, the jury announces the winner of the match.

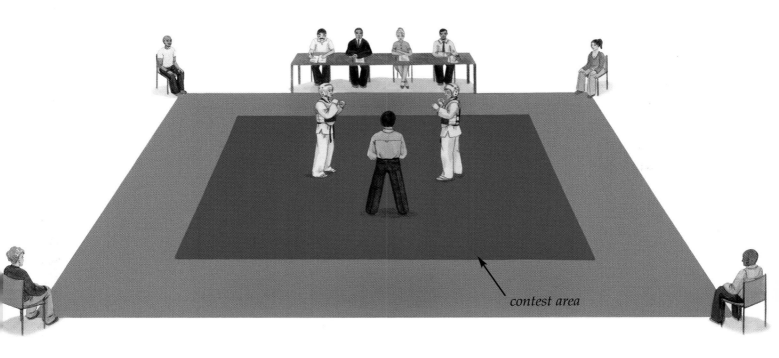

contest area

A competitor may receive warnings or deductions for many reasons, including striking an opponent on an illegal area of his or her body, grabbing hold of an opponent's uniform, and for showing anger.

31

Glossary

Note: Boldfaced words that are defined in the book may not appear in the glossary.

coordination The ability to perform more than one act at the same time

counterattack A return attack performed by an athlete immediately after he or she has been attacked

deflect To force an opponent's technique to move in another direction

flex To contract a muscle, causing a joint to bend

knife hand block A block performed with the hand in knife hand position

match A taekwondo competition between two students

opponent The person against whom a taekwondo athlete competes during competitions and sparring matches

rising block A block used against techniques aimed at the upper body

sabumnim A taekwondo instructor

self-discipline Control over one's own actions

stamina The strength to perform an act many times without feeling tired

stance A standing position made up of the positions of an athlete's feet, legs, and upper body

strike An action that involves an athlete hitting an opponent with part of his or her body

striking surface The part of an athlete's body that is used to strike an opponent

taekwondo master A taekwondo instructor with a fourth-degree or higher black belt

technique A taekwondo motion such as a punch or a kick

tunic A long, loose-fitting shirt

Index

1 2 3 4 5 6 7 8 9 0   Printed in the U.S.A.   4 3 2 1 0 9 8 7 6 5